family meals

Chef
express

Published by:
TRIDENT REFERENCE PUBLISHING
801 12th Avenue South, Suite 400
Naples, Fl 34102 USA

Tel: + 1 (239) 649-7077
www.tridentreference.com
email: sales@tridentreference.com

Family Meals
© TRIDENT REFERENCE PUBLISHING

Publisher
Simon St. John Bailey

Editor-in-chief
Susan Knightley

Prepress
Precision Prep & Press

Includes Index
ISBN 158279653X
UPC 6 15269 79653 5

Printed in The United States

introduction

Meal time, especially in the evening, is one of those rare moments of the day in which the family has a chance to get together. That's why this daily little feast deserves our best efforts put to work, to endow it with pleasant moments. A delicious meal, tempting and consistent at the same time, is the one to present to our loved ones.

family meals
introduction

From ancient times, the precedence order at the table has reflected the internal order of the family. Traditions that today are long lost would indicate who was to be served first, who second, as a way of establishing priorities by age and importance.
We could say that the family is formally constituted around the table. What is more, the sense of word home, which designates the house, which connotes family, is not complete without the domestic fire where the food was cooked.

- It is essential that everyday cooking meals be simple, nutritious, easy to make, tempting and suitable for all ages.
- Breads and cereals should not be missing from the daily diet, as they are the basis of the food chain.

- Pasta dishes are perfect when there are teenage members in the house, especially if they practice sports, as they provide carbohydrates, that are assimilated slowly and easily digestible at the same time.
- In the case of a large family, it's better to prepare very abundant dishes, storing individual portions in sealed packages. In time everyone can serve themselves to their liking. This is especially useful when there are children of various ages with diverse schedules and obligations. In this case a microwave oven is of great help, since it enables reheating food easily in a few minutes.
- A generous main dish, fruit or dessert are enough to compose a good homemade meal.
- Stews, soups and oven-cooked dishes are the most convenient, since they are easy to prepare and abundant, usually leaving every one satisfied.

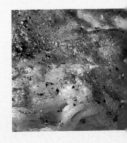

Difficulty scale

■☐☐ I Easy to do

■■☐ I Requires attention

■■■ I Requires experience

spaghetti
basil soup

■□□ | Cooking time: 27 minutes - Preparation time: 15 minutes

ingredients

> **155 g/5 oz spaghetti,** broken into pieces
> **2 tablespoons vegetable** oil
> **1 onion, chopped**
> **2 cloves garlic, crushed**
> **60 g/2 oz slivered** almonds
> **4 cups/1 liter/1³/4 pt** chicken stock
> **30 g/1 oz fresh basil** leaves, shredded
> **freshly ground black** pepper

method

1. Cook spaghetti in boiling water in a large saucepan following packet directions. Drain and set aside.
2. Heat oil in a large saucepan and cook onion, garlic and almonds, stirring over a medium heat for 6-7 minutes or until onions are transparent.
3. Add stock and basil to pan and bring to the boil, reduce heat, cover and simmer for 10 minutes. Stir in spaghetti and season to taste with black pepper. Spoon soup into bowls and serve immediately.

....
Serves 4

tip from the chef
This soup can be frozen because it does not contain eggs or cream. Basil should not be added before freezing the soup, but only on reheating, so that it maintains its properties.

vegetable
bean soup

■□□ | Cooking time: 45 minutes - Preparation time: 20 minutes

method

1. Heat oil in a large saucepan over a medium heat, add onions and cook, stirring, for 5 minutes or until onions are lightly browned.
2. Add carrots, potatoes and stock and bring to the boil. Reduce heat, cover and simmer for 30 minutes or until vegetables are tender.
3. Stir in beans, milk, dill, parsley and black pepper to taste and cook, stirring frequently, for 3-4 minutes or until heated through.

Serves 4

ingredients

> **2 tablespoons vegetable oil**
> **3 onions, diced**
> **3 carrots, diced**
> **3 potatoes, diced**
> **3 cups/750 ml/1^{1}/$_{4}$ pt vegetable stock**
> **315 g/10 oz canned cannellini beans, drained and rinsed**
> **^{1}/$_{2}$ cup/125 ml/4 fl oz milk**
> **2 tablespoons chopped fresh dill**
> **1 tablespoon chopped fresh parsley**
> **freshly ground black pepper**

tip from the chef

It can be served with croûtons (bread cubes, toasted or fried in oil or butter).

minestrone

■ ■ ■ | Cooking time: 95 minutes - Preparation time: 55 minutes

ingredients

> **2 tablespoons/60 g/2 oz butter**
> **2 cloves garlic, crushed**
> **2 small onions, finely chopped**
> **4 rashers bacon, chopped**
> **250 g/8 oz bacon bones**
> **150 g/4 1/2 oz red kidney beans**
> **100 g/3 1/2 oz haricot beans, soaked overnight**
> **1/2 small cabbage, roughly chopped**
> **100 g/3 1/2 oz spinach, washed and chopped**
> **3 medium-sized potatoes, peeled and chopped**
> **2 medium-sized carrots, peeled and diced**
> **150 g/4 1/2 oz fresh (or frozen) peas, shelled**
> **1 stalk celery, chopped**
> **2 tablespoons parsley, finely chopped**
> **2 liters/3 1/2 pt chicken stock**
> **salt to taste**
> **100 g/3 1/2 oz tomato and cheese tortellini**
> **50 g/2 oz pasta of your choice**
> **fresh Parmesan cheese**

method

1. Heat butter and add garlic, onion, bacon and bones. Sauté 4-5 minutes.
2. Add all other ingredients except pasta and bring to the boil. Allow to simmer, covered, for approximately 90 minutes.
3. Remove and discard bacon bones.
4. Stir in both pastas and cook until al dente.

....

Serves 4

tip from the chef

To serve, sprinkle with a generous helping of Parmesan and a good crusty loaf of your favorite bread.

three quick
pasta sauces

■□□ | Cooking time: 10 minutes - Preparation time: 10 minutes

method

1. To make tuna sauce, melt butter in a saucepan, add flour and cook for 1 minute. Blend stock and tuna liquid, stirring over medium heat until sauce boils and thickens. Reduce heat and add olives and lemon juice. Season to taste and stir well to combine. Break up tuna into smaller chunks and fold through sauce. Cook for 2-3 minutes. Spoon over hot pasta and serve.

2. To make seafood sauce, heat oil in a saucepan and cook onions for 1 minute. Stir in seafood and cook for 2 minutes longer. Combine tomatoes and wine and pour into pan. Bring to the boil, then reduce heat and simmer, uncovered, for 10 minutes. Add basil and spoon over hot pasta.

3. To make mushroom sauce, heat oil in a frying pan and cook bacon for 3-4 minutes or until crisp. Stir in mushrooms and cook for 2-3 minutes. Pour in cream, bring to the boil, stirring frequently, and simmer for 5 minutes or until sauce thickens. Season to taste, spoon over hot pasta, sprinkle with parsley and serve.

Serves 4

ingredients

tuna and olive sauce

> 30 g/2 oz butter
> 2 tablespoons flour
> 150 ml/5 fl oz chicken stock
> 440 g/14 oz tuna in brine, drained and liquid reserved
> 12 black olives, pitted and sliced
> 2 tablespoons lemon juice

seafood and tomato sauce

> 1 tablespoon olive oil
> 4 spring onions, finely chopped
> 500 g/1 lb assorted seafood, cooked and chopped
> 440 g/14 oz canned tomatoes, undrained and mashed
> 1/2 cup dry white wine
> 1 tablespoon chopped fresh basil

mushroom and bacon sauce

> 2 teaspoons olive oil
> 4 rashers bacon, chopped
> 125 g/4 oz button mushrooms, sliced
> 300 ml/9 fl oz cream (double)
> 1 tablespoon chopped fresh parsley

tip from the chef

For another super quick sauce, heat olive oil with aromatic herbs and condiments: basil, thyme, tarragon, coriander, garlic.

bows with
rich tomato basil sauce

■□□ I Cooking time: 30 minutes - Preparation time: 15 minutes

ingredients
> 185 g/6 oz bow pasta

tomato basil sauce
> 2 teaspoons olive oil
> 1 onion, sliced
> 1 clove garlic, crushed
> 3 tomatoes, peeled, seeded and chopped
> 125 ml/4 fl oz chicken stock
> 1 tablespoon tomato purée
> 1 tablespoon chopped fresh basil
> 2 teaspoons chopped fresh parsley
> 1/2 teaspoon sugar
> freshly ground black pepper
> grated Parmesan cheese

method
1. Cook pasta in boiling water in a saucepan following packet directions. Drain, set aside and keep warm.
2. To make sauce, heat oil in a saucepan and cook onion and garlic over a medium heat for 3-4 minutes or until onion is soft. Add tomatoes, stock, tomato purée, basil, parsley and sugar and simmer for 10-15 minutes or until reduced and thickened. Season to taste with black pepper. Spoon sauce over pasta. Sprinkle with a little grated fresh Parmesan cheese and extra chopped fresh basil.

Serves 2

tip from the chef
Any leftover sauce can be made into soup. To make, chop 1 small carrot and 1 stalk celery. Place leftover sauce, 250 ml/8 fl oz chicken stock, carrot and celery in a saucepan. Bring to simmering and simmer for 10-15 minutes or until carrot is tender. Season to taste with black pepper.

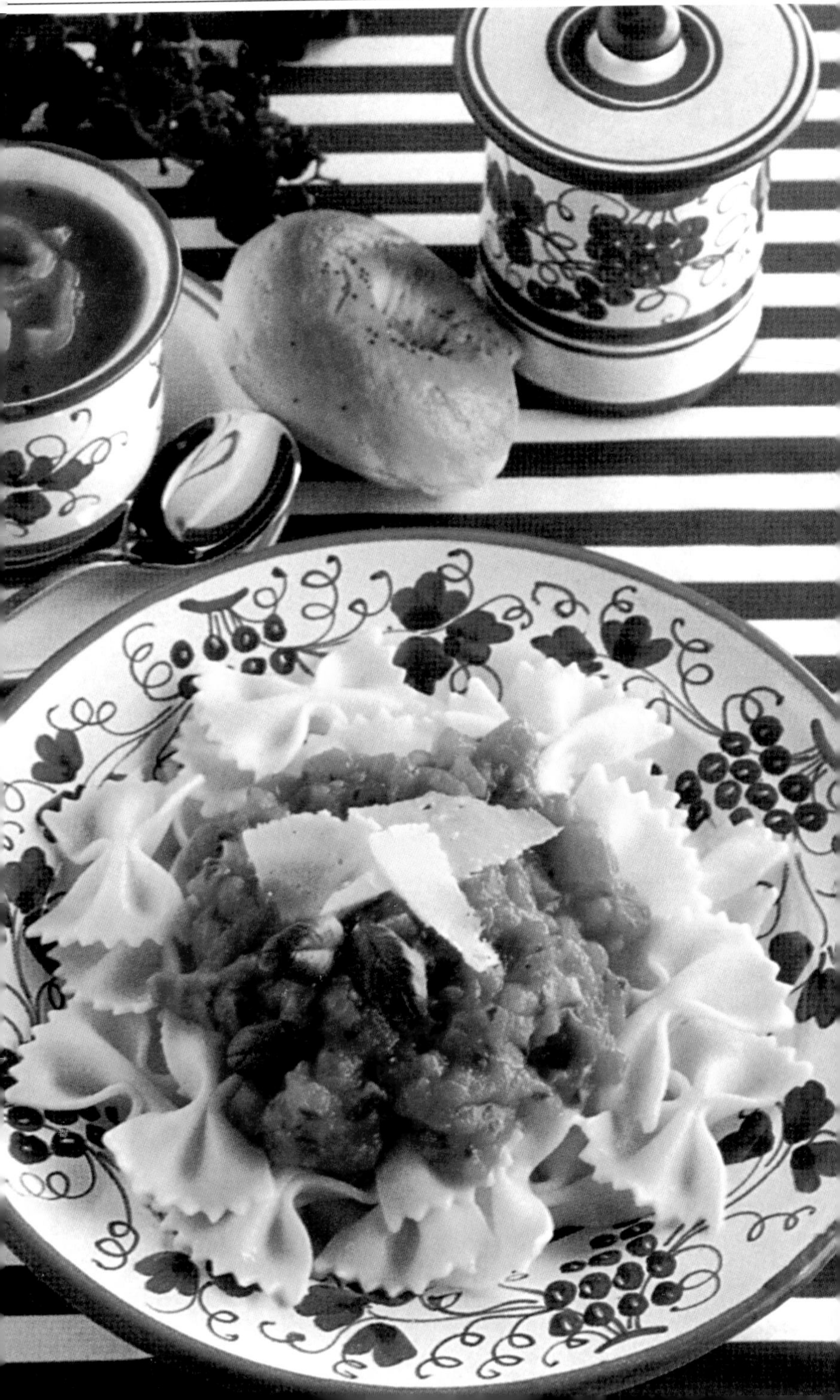

cheesy noodles

■□□ | Cooking time: 15 minutes - Preparation time: 5 minutes

method

1. Prepare noodles according to packet directions. Drain, add sour cream and black pepper to taste and toss to combine.
2. Divide noodle mixture between two heatproof serving dishes and sprinkle with cheese. Place under a preheated hot grill and cook for 3-4 minutes until cheese melts and is golden.

....
Serves 2

ingredients

> **2 x 90 g/3 oz packets quick-cooking noodles**
> **4 tablespoons sour cream**
> **freshly ground black pepper**
> **60 g/2 oz tasty cheese (mature Cheddar), grated**

tip from the chef

Accompany with a salad made of the lettuce or lettuces of your choice, cherry tomatoes, chopped or sliced red or green peppers and chopped or sliced cucumber tossed with a French dressing. Mixtures of fresh salad greens are available from many greengrocers and supermarkets. These are an economical and easy alternative to buying a variety of lettuces and making your own salads of mixed lettuce leaves.

spicy rice tomato and vegetables

■ ■ □ | Cooking time: 40 minutes - Preparation time: 20 minutes

method

1. Heat oil in a large saucepan. Cook onion, green pepper and chili for 3-4 minutes. Add rice, mix well and cook for 3-4 minutes.
2. Add tomatoes to the pan with stock or water. Bring to the boil and simmer for 30 minutes or until liquid is absorbed and rice is tender. Season with pepper.

Serves 4

ingredients

> 1 tablespoon olive oil
> 1 onion, sliced
> 1 green pepper, diced
> 1 red chili, seeded and finely chopped
> 3/4 cup/170 g/6 oz white rice
> 3/4 cup/170 g/6 oz quick-cooking brown rice
> 400 g/13 oz canned peeled tomatoes, undrained and roughly chopped
> 1 1/2 cups/375 ml/ 12 fl oz vegetable stock or water
> freshly ground black pepper

tip from the chef

For this recipe to be really exquisite, add a handful of peeled shrimp 5 minutes before cooking is done. Shrimp shells can be boiled in low heat to obtain an excellent broth.

potato gratin

■□□ | Cooking time: 45 minutes - Preparation time: 10 minutes

method

1. Layer potatoes, onions, chives and black pepper to taste in six lightly greased individual ovenproof dishes.
2. Place yogurt and cream in a bowl and mix to combine. Carefully pour yogurt mixture over potatoes and sprinkle with Parmesan cheese. Bake at 180°C/350°F/Gas 4 for 45 minutes or until potatoes are tender and top is golden.

....
Serves 6

ingredients

> **1 kg/2 lb potatoes, thinly sliced**
> **2 large onions, thinly sliced**
> **2 tablespoons snipped fresh chives**
> **freshly ground black pepper**
> **1¹/4 cup/250 g/ 8 oz low fat natural yogurt**
> **1 cup/250 ml/8 fl oz cream (heavy)**
> **60 g/2 oz grated Parmesan cheese**

tip from the chef

Instead of the cream yogurt sauce, make a bechamel with 2 tablespoons butter, 2 tablespoons flour and 400 cc/13 fl oz milk.

spinach
roulade

■ ■ ■ | Cooking time: 16 minutes - Preparation time: 35 minutes

ingredients

> **250 g/8 oz frozen spinach, thawed**
> **1 tablespoon plain flour**
> **5 eggs, separated**
> **15 g/¹/2 oz butter**
> **1 teaspoon ground nutmeg**
> **freshly ground black pepper**
> **2 tablespoons Parmesan cheese**

mushroom filling

> **30 g/1 oz butter**
> **100 g/3¹/2 oz button mushrooms, sliced**
> **3 spring onions, chopped**
> **440 g/14 oz canned peeled tomatoes, drained and chopped**
> **¹/2 teaspoon dried oregano**
> **¹/2 teaspoon dried basil**

method

1. Place spinach, flour, egg yolks, butter, nutmeg and black pepper to taste (a) in a food processor or blender and process until combined. Transfer to a bowl.
2. Beat egg whites until stiff peaks form, then mix 2 tablespoons of egg whites (b) into spinach mixture. Fold remaining egg whites into spinach mixture.
3. Spoon into a greased and lined Swiss roll tin (c) and bake at 200°C/400°F/Gas 6 for 12 minutes or until mixture is firm.
4. To make filling, melt butter in a frying pan and cook mushrooms over a medium heat for 1 minute. Add spring onions, tomatoes, oregano and basil and cook for 3 minutes longer.
5. Turn roulade out onto a teatowel sprinkled with Parmesan cheese and roll up. Allow to stand for 1 minute. Unroll and spread with filling. Reroll and serve immediately.

....

Serves 6

tip from the chef

For a complete meal, serve rice cream with maple syrup as a dessert. Mix 315 g/10 oz cooked short-grain rice with 300 ml/9¹/2 fl oz double cream, whipped, and 1 teaspoon ground cinnamon. Spoon into individual serving dishes and chill. Serve topped with maple syrup.

a

b

c

cauliflower
au gratin

■□□ | Cooking time: 30 minutes - Preparation time: 10 minutes

method

1. Steam, boil or microwave cauliflower until just tender. Drain and set aside.
2. Place milk in a saucepan and cook over a medium heat until almost boiling point. Remove pan from heat and stir in cornflour mixture. Return pan to heat and cook over a medium heat until sauce boils and thickens, stirring constantly (a).
3. Combine mustard and yogurt. Remove sauce from heat and blend in yogurt mixture. Season to taste with black pepper. Spread half the sauce over the base of an ovenproof dish. Top with cauliflower (b) and remaining sauce.
4. Combine cornflakes, cheese and butter. Sprinkle on top of cauliflower. Dust lightly with paprika and bake at 180°C/350°F/Gas 4 for 15-20 minutes or until golden brown.

Serves 4

ingredients

> 1 small cauliflower, broken into florets
> 375 ml/12 fl oz milk
> 1 1/2 tablespoons cornflour blended with 3 tablespoons water
> 1 teaspoon wholegrain mustard
> 3 tablespoons natural yogurt
> freshly ground black pepper
> 60 g/2 oz crushed cornflakes
> 3 tablespoons grated mature Cheddar
> 15 g/1/2 oz butter, melted
> paprika

tip from the chef

The ideal companion for barbecued or oven roasted chicken.

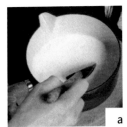

a

b

grilled
cod and potatoes

■□□ | Cooking time: 20 minutes - Preparation time: 10 minutes

ingredients

> **3 tablespoons olive oil**
> **2 tablespoons lime juice**
> **1 teaspoon crushed black peppercorns**
> **4 cod cutlets**
> **6 potatoes, very thinly sliced**
> sea salt

method

1. Preheat barbecue to a medium heat. Place 1 tablespoon oil, lime juice and black peppercorns in a bowl and mix to combine. Brush oil mixture over fish and marinate at room temperature for 10 minutes.
2. Brush potatoes with oil and sprinkle with salt. Place potatoes on lightly oiled barbecue grill and cook for 5 minutes each side or until tender and golden. Move potatoes to side of barbecue to keep warm.
3. Place fish on lightly oiled barbecue grill and cook for 3-5 minutes each side or until flesh flakes when tested with a fork. To serve, arrange potatoes attractively on serving plates and top with fish.

....

Serves 4

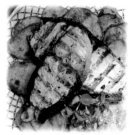

tip from the chef
Fish should be bought very fresh. When it is purchased frozen, be sure the cold storage has not been suspended; the packages need to be clean and ice-free on the inside.

salmon cutlets
with pineapple salsa

■□□ | Cooking time: 10 minutes - Preparation time: 25 minutes

method

1. Preheat barbecue to a medium heat. Cook salmon cutlets on lightly oiled barbecue for 3-5 minutes each side or until flesh flakes when tested with a fork.
2. To make salsa, place pineapple, spring onions, chili, lemon juice and mint in a food processor or blender and process to combine. Serve at room temperature with salmon cutlets.

Serves 4

ingredients

> 4 salmon cutlets, cut 2^1/$_2$ cm/1 in thick

pineapple salsa

> 250 g/8 oz roughly chopped fresh pineapple
> 2 spring onions, finely chopped
> 1 fresh red chili, seeded and finely chopped
> 1 tablespoon lemon juice
> 2 tablespoons finely chopped fresh mint

tip from the chef

If fresh pineapple is unavailable use canned crushed pineapple in natural juice, drained, in its place. This salsa is delicious served with any fish or barbecued chicken.

snapper fillets with
lemon and coriander

■□□ | Cooking time: 8 minutes - Preparation time: 5 minutes

ingredients

> 1 teaspoon chopped fresh ginger
> 1 teaspoon crushed garlic
> 2 tablespoons finely chopped coriander
> 2 tablespoons olive oil
> 1½ tablespoon lemon juice
> 500 g/1 lb snapper fillets (4 portions)

method

1. Mix the first 5 ingredients together in a shallow dish. Place the fillets in the dish and turn to coat well. Cover and stand 10-15 minutes.

2. Heat the barbecue to medium/hot and oil the grill bars. Place a sheet of baking paper over the bars and make a few slashes between the grill bars to allow ventilation. Place the fish on the paper and cook for 3-4 minutes each side according to thickness. Brush with marinade during cooking. Remove to plate. Heat any remaining marinade and pour over the fish.

Serves 4

tip from the chef

Fish is cooked, if when tested with a fork, it flakes or the sections pull away. Lingfish, haddock and perch may also be used.

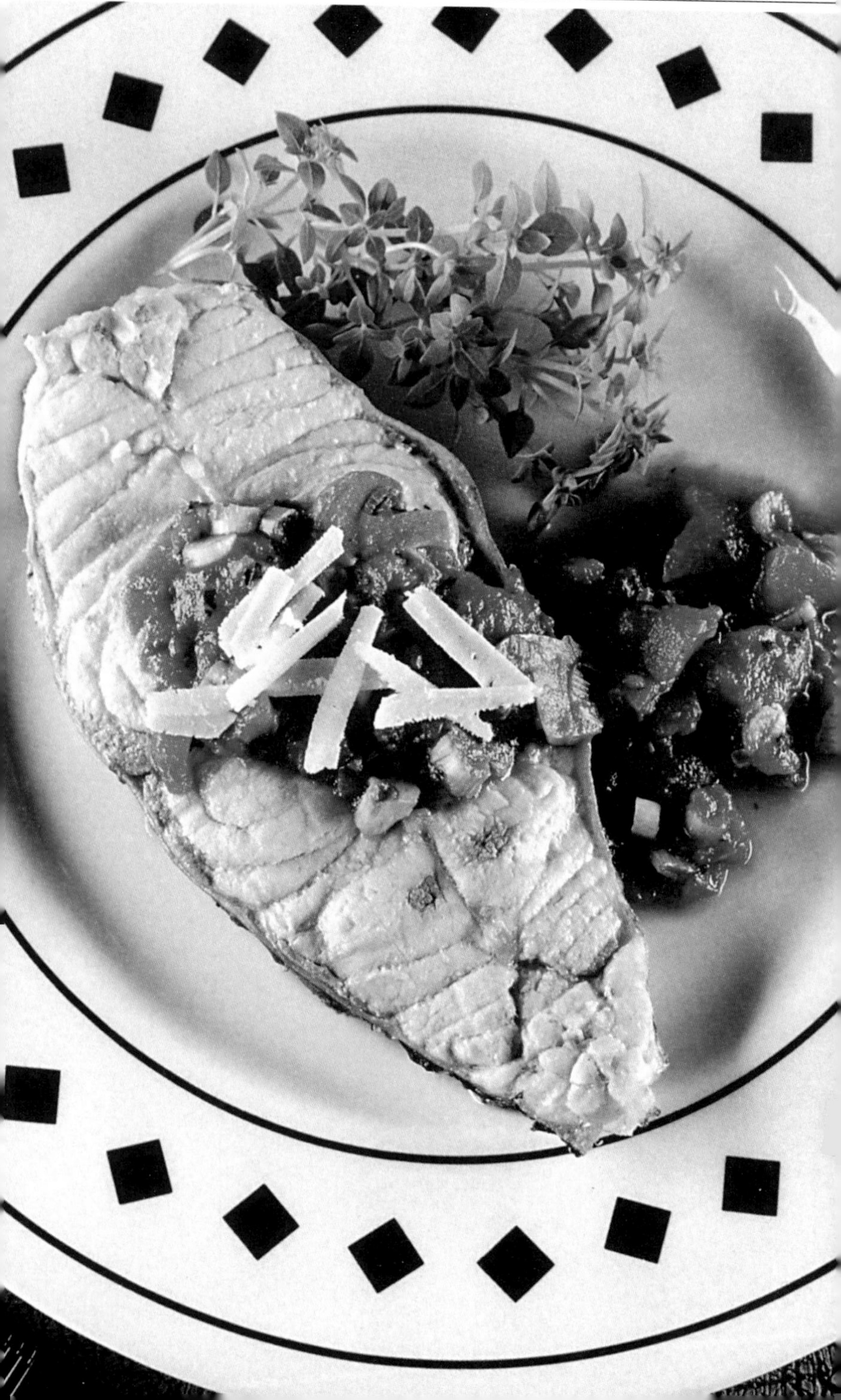

fish with
italian sauce

■□□ | Cooking time: 20 minutes - Preparation time: 15 minutes

method

1. Brush fish cutlets with lemon juice. Place under preheated grill and cook for 4-5 minutes each side. Remove from grill and keep warm.
2. Place shallots, garlic, tomatoes, mushrooms, wine, basil, oregano and pepper to taste in a saucepan. Bring to the boil, reduce heat and simmer gently for 8-10 minutes.
3. Arrange fish cutlets on serving plates. Spoon sauce over and top with Parmesan cheese.

Serves 4

ingredients

> 4 x 150 g white fish cutlets
> 2 tablespoons lemon juice
> 6 shallots, finely chopped
> 1 clove garlic, crushed
> 400 g/13$^{1}/_{2}$ oz canned tomatoes
> 200 g/7 oz button mushrooms, sliced
> $^{1}/_{2}$ cup/125 ml/4 fl oz red wine
> 2 teaspoons finely chopped fresh basil
> $^{1}/_{2}$ teaspoon dried oregano
> freshly ground black pepper
> 2 tablespoons grated Parmesan cheese

tip from the chef

For a crispy effect, combine equal parts of Parmesan chesse (finely grated) and breadcrumbs. Spread over fish and gratin under oven grill.

chicken
pot pie

■■■ I Cooking time: 50 minutes - Preparation time: 45 minutes

ingredients

> 60 g/2 oz butter
> 1 large onion, chopped
> 4 chicken breast fillets, cut into 2 cm/³/4 in cubes
> 2 potatoes, cut into 1 cm/1/2 in cubes
> 2 large carrots, cut into 1 cm/1/2 in cubes
> 1/4 cup/30 g/1 oz flour
> 1 cup/250 ml/8 fl oz dry white wine
> 3 cups/750 ml/1 1/4 pt chicken stock
> 1 cup/250 ml/8 fl oz cream (double)
> 2 tablespoons tomato paste (purée)

herbed scone topping

> 2 cups/250 g/8 oz self-raising flour, sifted
> 1 teaspoon dried mixed herbs
> 30 g/1 oz grated fresh Parmesan cheese
> 30 g/1 oz butter, chopped
> 1 cup/250 ml/8 fl oz milk

method

1. Melt butter in a large frying pan and cook onion, stirring, over a medium heat for 3-4 minutes or until onion is soft. Add chicken and cook, stirring, for 3 minutes longer.

2. Add potatoes and carrots and cook, stirring, for 8-10 minutes. Stir in flour, then wine, stock, cream and tomato paste (purée), and bring to simmering. Simmer for 10 minutes then transfer mixture to a casserole dish.

3. To make topping, place flour, herbs, Parmesan cheese and butter in a food processor and process to combine. With machine running, add milk and process to form a sticky dough. Turn dough onto a lightly floured surface and knead until smooth. Press dough out to 2 cm/³/4 in thick and, using a scone cutter, cut out rounds and place on top of casserole.

4. Bake at 200°C/400°F/Gas 6 for 20-25 minutes or until topping is cooked and golden, and casserole is hot.

....
Serves 4

tip from the chef

A delicious herb topping is an imaginative alternative to potatoes in this cobbler-style recipe. Serve with a green vegetable, such as beans, spinach or cabbage, for a complete meal.

thigh steaks
in fruity mint salsa

■□□ I Cooking time: 9 minutes - Preparation time: 15 minutes

method
1. Pound thigh fillets on both sides with a meat mallet to flatten. Sprinkle with salt (if using), pepper and oregano.
2. Heat a nonstick frying pan and lightly spray with oil, place in the thigh steaks and cook for 3 minutes on each side. Remove to a heated plate and keep hot.
3. Add diced pear, banana, lemon juice, mint and chili sauce to the pan. Scrape up pan juices and stir to heat fruit.
4. Pile hot fruit salsa on top of thigh steaks. Serve immediately with mashed potatoes or rice.

Serves 3-4

ingredients
> 500 g/1 lb chicken thigh fillets
> canola oil spray
> salt, pepper to taste (optional)
> $1/2$ teaspoon dried oregano
> 1 pear, peeled and diced
> 1 banana, peeled and diced
> 2 tablespoons lemon juice
> 3 tablespoons finely chopped mint
> 2 teaspoons sweet chili sauce

tip from the chef
Chicken meat goes with all condiments and sauces. Such versatility allows you to prepare anything from hearty winter meals, to this lighter spring dish.

roast turkey

■ ■ ■ | Cooking time: 3 1/2 hours - Preparation time: 70 minutes

ingredients

> **4 kg/8 lb turkey**
> **60 g/2 oz butter, melted**
> **250 ml/8 fl oz chicken stock**

veal forcemeat

> **30 g/1 oz butter**
> **1 onion, finely chopped**
> **1 rasher bacon, chopped**
> **250 g/8 oz veal mince**
> **185 g/6 oz breadcrumbs**
> **1/2 teaspoon finely grated lemon rind**
> **1 tablespoon finely chopped fresh parsley**
> **1/2 teaspoon dried sage**
> **pinch ground nutmeg**
> **freshly ground black pepper**
> **1 egg, lightly beaten**

chestnut stuffing

> **440 g/14 oz canned chestnut purée, sieved**
> **2 cooking apples, cored, peeled and grated**
> **185 g/6 oz breadcrumbs**
> **1 onion, chopped**
> **1 stalk celery, chopped**
> **4 tablespoons chopped walnuts**
> **45 g/1 1/2 oz butter, melted**
> **1 tablespoon finely chopped fresh parsley**
> **pinch ground nutmeg**
> **1 egg, lightly beaten**

method

1. To make forcemeat, melt butter in a frying pan and cook onion and bacon (a) for 4-5 minutes or until bacon is crisp. Add veal, breadcrumbs, lemon rind, parsley, sage, nutmeg, black pepper to taste and egg. Mix well to combine.

2. To make stuffing, combine chestnut purée, apples, breadcrumbs, onion, celery, walnuts, parsley, butter, black pepper to taste, nutmeg and egg.

3. Remove giblets and neck from turkey. Wipe turkey inside and out and dry well. Place stuffing in body cavity and lightly fill neck end of turkey with forcemeat (b). Secure openings with metal skewers and truss legs (c) and wings.

4. Place turkey on a roasting rack in a baking dish. Brush turkey with butter, then pour chicken stock into dish. Bake at 180°C/350°F/Gas 4 for 3-3 1/2 hours or until tender. Baste frequently with pan juices during cooking. Set aside to stand for 20 minutes before carving.

....

Serves 10

tip from the chef

The Spaniards brought turkeys to Europe from North America in the 1520s. Cooks soon developed wonderful dishes for special occasions with delicious stuffings and accompaniments. Try this roast turkey for Christmas or Thanksgiving dinner.

a

b

c

barbecued chicken
and mushroom patties

■ □ □ | Cooking time: 16 minutes - Preparation time: 30 minutes

method

1. Place ground chicken meat in a large bowl and add remaining ingredients (a) except oil. Mix well to combine ingredients, then knead a little with one hand to make the meat fine in texture. With wet hands, shape into 4 or 5 flat patties (b).
2. Heat barbecue or grill to medium-high. Spray grill bars or rack with a little oil and place on the patties (c). Cook for 8 minutes on each side or until cooked through. Patties are cooked when juices run clear after being pricked with a skewer.
3. Serve hot with vegetable accompaniments.

ingredients

> **500 g/1 lb ground chicken meat**
> **1/2 cup dried breadcrumbs**
> **1 medium onion, chopped**
> **1/2 teaspoon salt**
> **1/2 teaspoon pepper**
> **2 tablespoons lemon juice**
> **2 tablespoons chopped parsley**
> **1/2 cup finely chopped mushrooms**
> **vegetable oil**

....
Serves 4-5

tip from the chef

For quick preparation place onion, parsley and mushrooms in a food processor and chop together. May be cooked on flat-top barbecue, electric table grill or conventional gas or electric grill.

a

b

c

lamb
and vegetable pot

■■☐ I Cooking time: 90 minutes - Preparation time: 45 minutes

ingredients

> **750 g/1¹/2 lb leg of lamb, cut into 2 cm/³/4 in cubes**
> **2 tablespoons seasoned flour**
> **15 g/¹/2 oz butter**
> **2 tablespoons oil**
> **6 baby onions, peeled and bases left intact**
> **6 baby new potatoes**
> **2 cloves garlic, crushed**
> **3 stalks celery, sliced**
> **1 red pepper, sliced**
> **2 rashers bacon, chopped**
> **1 carrot, sliced**
> **375 ml/12 fl oz beef stock**
> **125 ml/4 fl oz red wine**
> **1 tablespoon tomato purée**
> **2 tablespoons finely chopped fresh rosemary**
> **250 g/8 oz green beans, trimmed and cut into 2.5 cm/1 in lengths**
> **1 tablespoon cornflour blended with 2 tablespoons water**
> **freshly ground black pepper**

method

1. Toss meat in flour. Heat butter and 1 tablespoon oil in a large heavy-based saucepan and cook meat in batches (a) until brown on all sides. Remove from pan and set aside.

2. Heat remaining oil in pan and cook onions and potatoes until brown on all sides. Remove from pan and set aside. Add garlic, celery, red pepper and bacon (b) and cook for 4-5 minutes. Return meat, onions and potatoes to pan. Mix in carrot, stock, wine (c), tomato purée and rosemary. Bring to the boil, then reduce heat and simmer, covered, for 1 hour or until meat is tender. Stir in beans and cornflour mixture, season to taste with black pepper and cook for 10 minutes longer.

....
Serves 6

tip from the chef
A whole leg lamb can be larded with garlic and rosemary, and roasted in the oven.

a

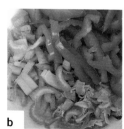

b

c

family roast

■ ■ ■ | Cooking time: 2¹/2 hours - Preparation time: 60 minutes

method

1. Place beef on a wire rack set in a flameproof roasting dish or tin. Brush beef with 1 tablespoon oil and sprinkle with black pepper to taste. Bake at 210°C/420°F/Gas 7 for 1-1¹/4 hours for medium rare or until cooked to your liking.

2. For vegetables, place potatoes, pumpkin or parsnips and onions in a large saucepan, cover with water and bring to the boil. Reduce heat and simmer for 3 minutes, then drain. Arrange vegetables in a baking dish and brush with ¹/4 cup/60ml/2fl oz oil. Bake, turning once during cooking, for 45 minutes or until vegetables are tender and browned.

3. To make gravy, transfer roast to a serving platter, cover with foil and rest for 15 minutes. Stir wine or stock, mushrooms, tarragon and black pepper to taste into meat juices in roasting dish or tin and place over a medium heat. Bring to the boil, stirring to loosen sediment, then reduce heat and simmer until sauce reduces and thickens. Slice beef and serve with vegetables and gravy.

ingredients

> 1¹/2 kg/3 lb piece fresh round beef
> 1 tablespoon olive oil
> freshly ground black pepper

roast vegetables

> 6 large potatoes, halved
> 6 pieces pumpkin or 3 parsnips, halved
> 6 onions, peeled
> ¹/4 cup/60 ml/2 fl oz olive oil

mushroom gravy

> 1 cup/250 ml/8 fl oz red wine or beef stock
> 60 g/2 oz button mushrooms, sliced
> ¹/2 teaspoon dried tarragon

Serves 6-8

tip from the chef

Another alternative to the mushroom sauce is a home-made mayonnaise: beat 1 egg, add a few drops of lemon and 1 cup oil in a thin stream. Add salt and blend till it thickens.

italian
sausage and pork roll

■■□ | Cooking time: 80 minutes - Preparation time: 40 minutes

ingredients

> **500 g/1 lb lean pork mince**
> **250 g/8 oz Italian sausages, casings removed**
> **1 onion, chopped**
> **1/2 chicken stock cube**
> **2 slices white bread, crusts removed**
> **2 tablespoons tomato paste (purée)**
> **1 egg, lightly beaten**
> **freshly ground black pepper**
> **250 g/8 oz ricotta cheese, drained**
> **2 tablespoons chopped fresh basil**
> **4 slices pancetta or bacon, chopped**
> **1 red pepper, roasted and sliced**
> **60 g/2 oz pepperoni sausage, chopped**
> **4 black olives, sliced**
> **4 canned anchovy fillets, chopped**
> **2 hard-boiled eggs, quartered**
> **1 tablespoon olive oil**
> **2 tablespoons brown sugar**
> **1 teaspoon dried fennel seeds**
> **1/2 teaspoon dried rosemary**

method

1. Place pork, sausage meat, onion, stock cube, bread, tomato paste (purée), egg and black pepper to taste in a food processor and process to combine. Press out meat mixture on a large piece of aluminum foil (a) to form a 20 x 30 cm/8 x 12 in rectangle.

2. Spread meat with ricotta cheese and sprinkle with basil. Top with pancetta or bacon, red pepper, pepperoni, olives, anchovies and hard-boiled eggs (b), then roll up like a Swiss roll and wrap in foil (c). Place on a baking tray and bake at 180°C/350°F/Gas 4 for 40 minutes. Remove foil and drain off juices.

3. Place unwrapped roll back on baking tray and brush with oil. Combine sugar, fennel seeds and rosemary, sprinkle over roll and bake for 40 minutes longer or until cooked.

....

Serves 6

tip from the chef

Of Italian origin, pancetta is a type of bacon available from the delicatessen section of your supermarket or Italian food shop.

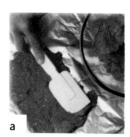

a

b

c

scotch meatballs

■■□ | Cooking time: 6 minutes - Preparation time: 40 minutes

method

1. Place mince, parsley and curry powder in a bowl and mix to combine. Divide mixture into four equal portions. Place each portion on a piece of plastic food wrap and press into a 12 cm/5 in circle.

2. Combine milk and egg in a shallow dish. Dip hard-boiled eggs into milk mixture then roll in flour to coat. Place an egg in the center of each mince circle and mould around egg to enclose (a). Dip wrapped egg in milk mixture (b), then roll in breadcrumbs to coat.

3. Heat oil in a saucepan until a cube of bread dropped in browns in 50 seconds. Deep-fry meatballs, two at a time, for 5-6 minutes or until golden. Drain on absorbent kitchen paper and cool completely. Cut in half to serve.

....
Makes 8 halves

ingredients

> **500 g/1 lb sausage mince**
> **2 tablespoons chopped fresh parsley**
> **1 teaspoon curry powder**
> **1/2 cup/60 ml/2 fl oz milk**
> **1 egg, beaten**
> **4 hard-boiled eggs, peeled**
> **1/2 cup/60 g/2 oz flour**
> **1 cup/125 g/4 oz dried breadcrumbs**
> **vegetable oil for deep-frying**

a

b

tip from the chef

It's a good idea to serve these meatballs as a snack to go with a drink. In this case, make them smaller, using quail eggs. Cooking time will be shorter.

pork
and apple cabbage rolls

■ ■ ■ | Cooking time: 90 minutes - Preparation time: 55 minutes

ingredients

> **2 tablespoons vegetable oil**
> **1 onion, finely grated**
> **2 rashers bacon, chopped**
> **1 green apple, peeled, cored and grated**
> **1 teaspoon caraway seeds**
> **500 g/1 lb lean pork mince**
> **125 g/4 oz brown rice, cooked**
> **1 egg, lightly beaten**
> **freshly ground black pepper**
> **8 large cabbage leaves**
> **60 g/2 oz butter**
> **1¹/2 tablespoons paprika**
> **1¹/2 tablespoons flour**
> **1 tablespoon tomato paste (purée)**
> **¹/2 cup/125 ml/4 fl oz red wine**
> **1¹/2 cup/375 ml/12 fl oz chicken stock**
> **¹/2 cup/125 g/4 oz sour cream**

method

1. Heat oil in a frying pan over a medium heat, add onion and bacon and cook, stirring, for 3-4 minutes or until onion is soft. Stir in apple and caraway seeds and cook for 2 minutes longer. Remove pan from heat and set aside to cool.
2. Place pork, rice, egg, black pepper to taste and onion mixture in a bowl and mix to combine.
3. Boil, steam or microwave cabbage leaves until soft. Refresh under cold running water, pat dry with absorbent kitchen paper and trim stalks.
4. Divide meat mixture between cabbage leaves and roll up, tucking in sides. Secure with wooden toothpicks or cocktail sticks.
5. Melt 30 g/1 oz butter in a frying pan, add rolls and cook, turning several times, until lightly browned. Transfer rolls to a shallow ovenproof dish.
6. Melt remaining butter in pan over a medium heat, stir in paprika and flour and cook for 2 minutes. Stir in tomato paste (purée), wine and stock and bring to the boil. Reduce heat and simmer, stirring, for 5 minutes. Remove pan from heat and whisk in sour cream. Pour sauce over rolls, cover and bake at 180°C/350°F/Gas 4 for 1 hour.

....

Serves 4

tip from the chef

These rolls are also delicious when made using lamb mince instead of the pork. This recipe is a good way to use up leftover cooked rice and spinach. Silverbeet leaves can be used instead of cabbage.

apple
pork casserole

■ ■ □ | Cooking time: 80 minutes - Preparation time: 45 minutes

method

1. Heat butter in a large frying pan and cook onions and pork over a medium heat for 5 minutes. Add apples, herbs, stock and black pepper to taste, bring to the boil, then reduce heat and simmer for 1 hour or until pork is tender. Using a slotted spoon remove pork and set aside.
2. Push liquid and solids through a sieve and return to pan with pork.
3. To make sauce, melt butter in a frying pan and cook apple over a medium heat for 2 minutes. Stir in chives and tomatoes and bring to the boil, reduce heat and simmer for 5 minutes. Pour into pan with pork and cook over a medium heat for 5 minutes longer. Just prior to serving, sprinkle with cracked black peppercorns.

Serves 4

ingredients

> 30 g/1 oz butter
> 2 onions, chopped
> 500 g/1 lb lean diced pork
> 3 large apples, peeled, cored and chopped
> 1 tablespoon dried mixed herbs
> 3 cups/750 ml/1¼ pt chicken stock
> freshly ground black pepper

apple sauce

> 30 g/1 oz butter
> 2 apples, peeled, cored and chopped
> 2 tablespoons snipped fresh chives
> 440 g/14 oz canned tomatoes, undrained and mashed
> 1 teaspoon cracked black peppercorns

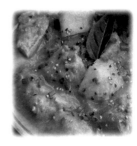

tip from the chef

1 cup apple jam can be used instead of the apple sauce.

french
vanilla ice milk base

■■□ | Cooking time: 8 minutes - Preparation time: 30 minutes

ingredients
> 4¹/4 cups/960 ml/
1¹/2 pt skim milk
> ³/4 cup/185 g/6 oz sugar
> 2 vanilla beans or 2
tablespoons vanilla
extract
> 2 egg yolks

method
1. In a heavy-based saucepan, heat milk, sugar, and vanilla bean. (If you are using vanilla extract, do not add it until step 4). Stir occasionally until sugar is dissolved and the mixture is hot but not boiling.
2. Whisk egg yolks together in a bowl. Continue whisking and very slowly pour in approximately 1 cup/250 ml/8 oz of the milk mixture. When smooth, pour back into the pan.
3. Whisk constantly over low heat until the mixture thickens slightly and coats the back of a spoon (about 5 minutes). Take care that the mixture doesn't boil, or it will curdle. Draw your finger across the back of the coated spoon. If the line you make remains, the custard is done.
4. Remove vanilla bean; or, if you're using vanilla extract, add it at this stage.
5. Strain into a clean bowl and cool thoroughly.
6. Transfer to an ice cream machine and freeze according to manufacturer's instructions.

Makes approximately 4 cups/900 ml/32 fl oz

tip from the chef
This recipe produces consistently excellent flavor and texture. Experiment to find which combination of ingredients is most appealing to your palate. Vanilla beans will give a richer flavor than extract.

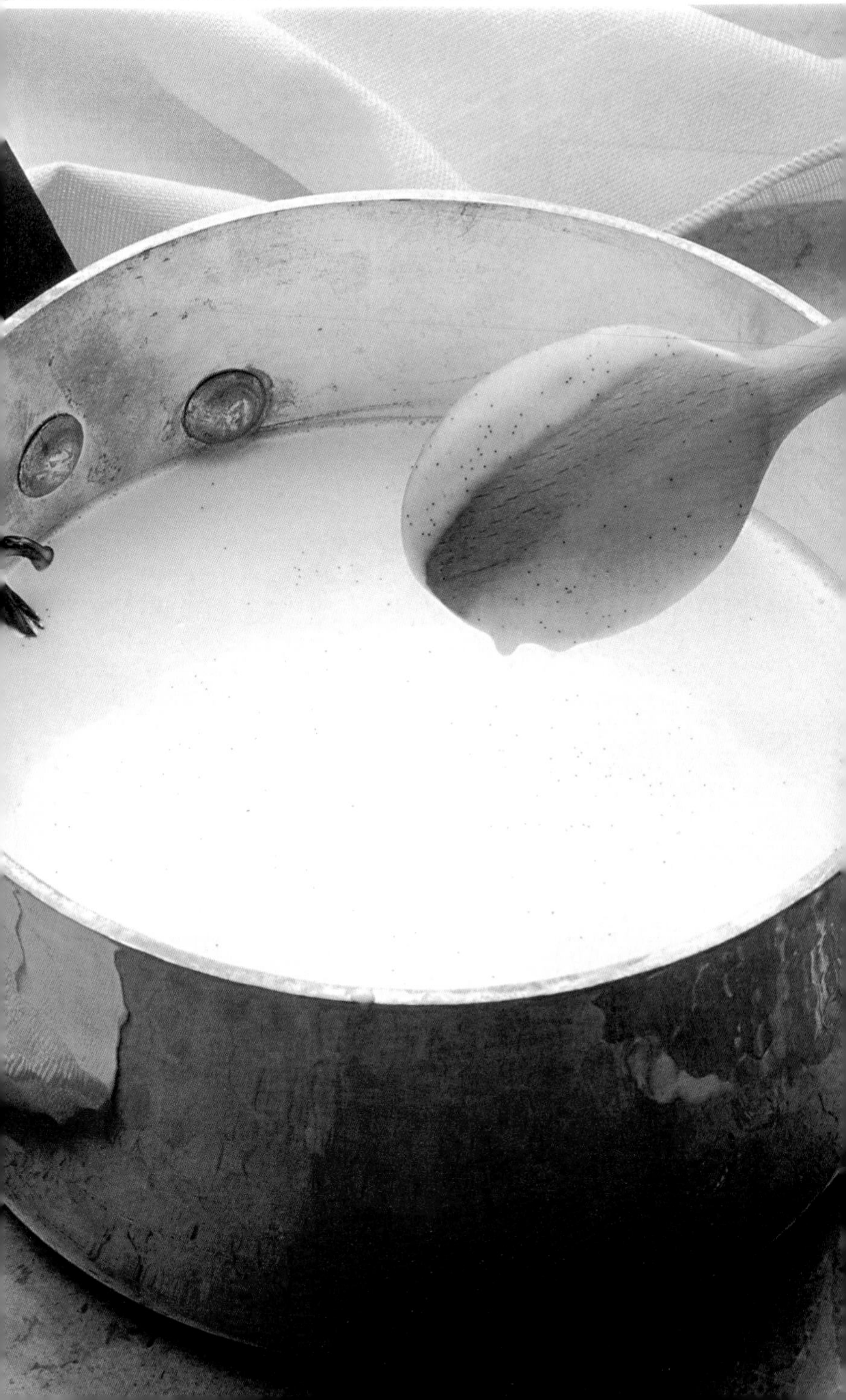

french
bread pudding

■ ■ □ | Cooking time: 70 minutes - Preparation time: 45 minutes

method

1. To make filling, place figs, dates, orange juice, brandy and cinnamon stick in a saucepan and cook over a low heat, stirring, for 15-20 minutes or until fruit is soft and mixture thick. Remove cinnamon stick.

2. To assemble pudding, place one-third of the brioche slices in the base of a greased 11 x 21 cm/4^1/$_2$ x 8^1/$_2$ in loaf tin. Top with half the filling. Repeat layers, ending with a layer of brioche.

3. Place eggs, milk, vanilla essence and nutmeg in a bowl and whisk to combine. Carefully pour egg mixture over brioche and fruit and set aside to stand for 5 minutes. Place tin in a baking dish with enough boiling water to come halfway up the sides of the tin and bake at 160°C/325°F/Gas 3 for 45 minutes or until firm. Stand pudding in tin for 10 minutes before turning out and serving.

ingredients

> 1 loaf brioche, sliced
> 6 eggs, lightly beaten
> 1^1/$_2$ cups/375 ml/ 12 fl oz milk
> 1 teaspoon vanilla essence
> 1 teaspoon ground nutmeg

fruit filling

> 125 g/4 oz dried figs, chopped
> 125 g/4 oz dried dates, pitted and chopped
> 1/2 cup/125 ml/4 fl oz orange juice
> 1/3 cup/90 ml/3 fl oz brandy
> 1 cinnamon stick

Serves 6-8

tip from the chef

This tempting dessert is better eaten cut into slices and served with cream shortly after it is turned out of the tin.

featherlight scones

■ ■ □ | Cooking time: 20 minutes - Preparation time: 35 minutes

ingredients

> **4 cups/500 g/1 lb self-raising flour, sifted**
> **2 tablespoons superfine sugar**
> **1/4 teaspoon salt**
> **60 g/2 oz butter**
> **1 cup/250 ml/8 fl oz buttermilk**
> **3/4 cup/185 ml/6 fl oz water**
> **milk for glazing**
> **jam or lemon curd**
> **whipped cream (optional)**

method

1. Place flour, sugar and salt in a bowl and mix to combine. Add chopped butter (a). Using fingertips, rub in butter until mixture resembles fine breadcrumbs. Add milk and water all at once and, using a rounded knife, mix lightly and quickly to make a soft, sticky dough.
2. Turn dough onto a lightly floured surface (b) and knead lightly until smooth. Press out to make 3 cm/1 1/4 in thick rectangle (c) and using a 5 cm/2 in scone cutter, cut out rounds.
3. Place scones, just touching, in a greased shallow 18 x 28 cm/7 x 11 in baking tin (d).
4. Brush with milk and bake at 220°C/425°F/Gas 7 for 12-15 minutes or until scones are well risen and golden. Transfer to wire racks to cool.
5. To serve, split scones and top with jam or lemon curd and cream, if desired.

....

Makes about 20

tip from the chef

Accompany these scones with a quick lemon sauce. Blend 1 cup cream cheese with 3 tablespoons honey, 1/2 teaspoon vanilla essence and 2 tablespoons lemon juice.

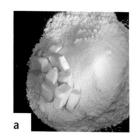

a

b

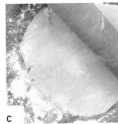

c

d

easy chocolate cake

a

■□□ | Cooking time: 45 minutes - Preparation time: 20 minutes

method

1. Place milk, butter and eggs (a) in a bowl and whisk to combine.
2. Sift together flour and cocoa powder (b) into a separate bowl. Add sugar and mix to combine. Make a well in the center of the dry ingredients and pour in milk mixture. Beat (c) for 5 minutes or until mixture is smooth.
3. Pour mixture into a greased 20 cm/8 in round cake tin (d) and bake at 180°C/350°F/Gas 4 for 40 minutes or until cooked when tested with a skewer. Stand cake in tin for 5 minutes before turning onto a wire rack to cool.
4. To make icing, sift icing sugar and cocoa powder together into a bowl. Stir in milk and mix until smooth. Spread icing over cold cake.

Makes a 20 cm/8 in round cake

ingredients

> **1 cup/250 ml/8 fl oz milk**
> **125 g/4 oz butter, softened**
> **2 eggs, lightly beaten**
> **1¹/₃ cups/170 g/5¹/₂ oz self-raising flour**
> **²/₃ cup/60 g/2 oz cocoa powder**
> **1 cup/220 g/7 oz caster sugar**

chocolate icing

> **1 cup/155 g/5 oz icing sugar**
> **2 tablespoons cocoa powder**
> **2 tablespoons milk**

tip from the chef

To make the cake richer, cut in two layers and fill with raspberry jam.

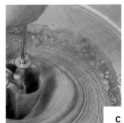

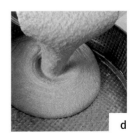

b   c   d

original
choc-chip cookies

■□□ | Cooking time: 15 minutes - Preparation time: 25 minutes

method

1. Place butter and sugar in a bowl and beat until light and fluffy. Beat in egg.
2. Add sifted flour, baking powder, coconut, chocolate chips and hazelnuts to butter mixture and mix to combine.
3. Drop tablespoons of mixture onto greased baking trays and bake at 180°C/350°F/Gas 4 for 12-15 minutes or until cookies are golden. Transfer to wire racks to cool.

....
Makes 35

ingredients

> **250 g/8 oz butter, softened**
> **1 cup/170 g/5¹/₂ oz brown sugar**
> **1 egg**
> **2 cups/250 g/6 oz plain flour**
> **1¹/₄ teaspoons baking powder**
> **45 g/1¹/₂ oz desiccated coconut**
> **220 g/7 oz chocolate chips**
> **185 g/6 oz hazelnuts, toasted, roughly chopped**

tip from the chef

Everyone's favorite biscuit, it is full of the flavor of coconut, toasted hazelnuts and a generous portion of chocolate chips!

index